Journey of a Radiant Heart

A WOMAN'S PERSPECTIVE ON SPIRITUAL ASCENSION, VOL I

NIOMI NICCI

Pasos Publishing House | Omi's Books

Journey of a radiant heart

The Stairway Trilogy^{TM} - vol I

Copyright © 2022-2024 by Niomi Nicci

Cover artwork by CA Pierce
Interior illustrations by Charlotte Thomson
Meditation sketches by Niomi Nicci

Published by Pasos Publishing House/ Omi's Books
ISBN: 979-8-218-00754-6

about. Words with a superscript^G have definitions in the glossary at the end of the book. Additional coaching and mentoring sections from my own personal healing work are also included.

Okay, now some tidbits about me.

Hi there, I'm NIOMI. I've spent much of my life working in hospital research. Most of those years were in a laboratory setting as a clinical microbiologist. I am not trained as a therapist, and I hold no degrees which allow me to advise people about energy work in any form. This book started as a journal, a diary of sorts. Just a way for me to track all the years of ascension work I've done. I like to call it volume one or the first installment of *The Stairway Trilogy*^{TM}.

I decided to share my life lessons with anyone going through an awakening of their own and attempting to navigate through a religion or just life itself. For me this was a journey that spanned out over twenty years. It started as a spiritual quest that took me into the Santeria religion and then out of it.

This book chronicles my ascension process, one where I walked out of the DARKNESS and into the LIGHT. Along the way, I encountered many spirit guides, amazing energy healers and even some off-world beings.

Preface

To all the angelic souls on earth
searching for enlightenment.
These pages are dedicated to your
healing and mine.

Introduction

A quick note on how the book is structured: Besides the chapter sections, which are pretty easy to follow, peppered throughout the chapters you will find "heart lockers." The information within them acts as a key to a higher vibration of thinking. They also function as a recap of the chapter or an intro for the next. Either way, just look at them as a friendly guide.

Also, I use the words "saint" and "*santo*" interchangeably throughout the book. I do the same with "the universe," "the source," "spirit," and "my higher self"; they all have the same meaning.

An *asterisk indicates a name and/or gender change to protect the identity of the other person I'm writing

If you're looking for advice from a licensed therapist or medical doctor, this is not the right book for you. If you're interested in learning tools for your own healing process,

WELCOME.

I'm finding my way again.

—NIOMI

Contents

Part One

OUT OF THE DARK

the awakening

~~

Coming off the Pelham Parkway 6 train, I walked two blocks, then down into a secluded basement in the South Bronx. Nervously, I waited to start the process of receiving my *elekes,* the sacred beads of the *orishas*[G]. As I waited for the elders to start the ceremony, I began contemplating my life decisions thus far. "It's the middle of January and freakin' cold," I mumbled to myself. *Have I seriously given enough consideration to the changes I'm about to make in my life? Do I really understand the consequences I will face if I go through this process? Do I really know what*

I'm getting myself into? Obviously, I wasn't ready.

Ten months later, I was initiated into the Santeria religion as a child of Yemaya. There was no turning back now. You know what people say: Hindsight is always 20/20. It has been twenty-one years since I was initiated, and while I no longer practice that religion, I do maintain a relationship with the *santos*. My bond with my orisha, my guardian saint, Yemaya, is eternal. She and I are one.

Before I continue into the depths of my experience, let me take you back to the beginning, where it all started. The journey that led me to Santeria, the world of *los santos*.

It was May 1992 and I had just returned from upstate New York, where I completed my first year of college. I felt like I had lost my confidence. Before I left, I had a clear idea of where I wanted my life and career to go. I knew I wanted to be a scientist and work in a laboratory.

However, those goals quickly dissolved. It was as though I had no direction, no motivation, no more life inside of me. I was drowning in a sea of confusion. And why? I'm not sure, but my journey into spiritual ascension definitely started there, what felt like a crossroads.

Being a middle child (there are four of us), I was always labeled the clear-headed one. Born and raised in New York City, I was used to juggling many tasks and maintaining a balance, with my high school classes and a budding musical side. Did I tell you? I was once an amazing pianist. In high school my greatest joy was being able to travel every year to a different state and compete in local piano and science fair competitions. Over four years I won about a thousand dollars and for a teenager that was like hitting the lotto. Before I left for college, I loved traveling into the city to listen to classical music and opera. First, I would treat myself to a twenty-dollar buffet-style meal at a restaurant on the Upper West Side.

Then I would walk over to the Metropolitan Opera House (the Met) or Lincoln Center for a show. I stopped playing when I left for school. My interests changed; there were other priorities then.

Both my parents were immigrants, arriving from the Caribbean with only the clothes on their backs. They made sacrifices that eventually allowed us to live a comfortable middle-class life. And, because of that, I really wanted to do well in school. I wasn't the most social person, but I did have a small group of friends that I hung out with in high school and they were equally ambitious. So of course, after that freshman year of college was unsuccessful, with a loss of concentration and having nearly failed all my classes, I made the difficult decision to move back to home.

What caused me to lose my edge? I would ask myself daily. I wasn't sure, but there was a block between me and my inner knowing. *Is there a negative energy around me? Is there a negative vibration or frequency I'm dealing with unknowingly?* Sometimes I would read about curses, people giving the evil eye to someone. *Is the loss of my inner confidence due to negative energy sent my way, intentionally or unintentionally?* That intuition that had protected me for years, I felt was no longer there.

I had been on my own, living on campus away from my family for the first time. Away from that "safety net" which had always given me a foundation, the only one I knew. Even though it had its own dysfunctions—sibling rivalry, verbal assaults—it still was the only sense of stability I had ever had. Now, I was consciously choosing to create a new foundation on my own, independent from an environment I felt at times was uncomfortable.

A few months after I returned to New York City, I started looking for ways to heal myself and find a sense of direction and focus once again. I began attending spiritual groups in Manhattan, going to metaphysical centers, and reading about Eastern medicine healing modalities like Reiki.

It was during that time I met Ms.*Cee Cee. She was a tall, statuesque African American spiritualist and energy healer. I went with a friend to her seminar in Manhattan. The first meeting was in a small, cramped meeting room, on the fourth floor of a building in the East Village. I remember the water bottle, tucked into a corner on the left-hand side of the room, just as we entered. There were about a dozen chairs all facing a large window, and in front and slightly off to the right side was a mobile chalkboard, although she didn't use chalk on it, more like an erasable marker.

It was a mixed crowd, but mostly, what seemed to me, young to middle-aged women. Ms. Cee Cee talked about self-empowerment, connecting to the spirit, and detoxification of the body. According to her teaching, the "mind, body, and spirit are one." If there are any disassociations between two or all three, it can cause confusion.

At the end of the seminar, we all got the chance to speak to her individually and draw cards from three different tarot decks. Then, we would receive a message from her guardian angel. I was quick to get up and take a spot behind a handful of people lined up single file. I thought of what we just spoke about during the seminar and then suddenly, it was my turn. I approached her, told her my name, and then chose the one most people avoided. I had always been the "odd" one in my family and here I was, one of the rare ones choosing from a pile of cards everyone else seemed to avoid but they felt familiar to me.

"AH!" she said. "Yes, you're different. Good for you; everyone seems to be avoiding this deck." Then she said,

"Choose three cards," at which time I pulled them and she began to channel information from her guide. I was told to pray and fast for forty days. After that time, I would receive a blessing from the spiritual realm, as I would be about to ascend.

Unsure what "ascension" meant, I just followed her guidance and thanked her. She also advised me to take a spiritual bath for forty days, using special oils like frankincense, which are believed to help promote peace and stability. That evening, I left with my friend and hopped on the E train back to Queens. I then proceeded to start praying and not eating or drinking from sunrise to sunset.

Three days into the fasting period, on May 3, 1993, I had my first visitation from an angel. I saw it descend with wings, touch me, and then ascend up toward the celestial world. What a truly amazing experience it was. It was then that I understood what ascension really meant, that I understood the power of prayer. Fortunately, my grandfather was visiting from the West Indies and as a priest in Shango Baptist, as it's known in the Caribbean, he helped me to understand what just happened. He explained that I had ascended to the level of the angel, which allowed me to see and feel it. I was relieved I had someone to discuss the experience with.

When I returned to Ms. Cee Cee and her wonderful insight, I explained in detail what happened and she said, "See? God said, 'Prove me—see if I won't pour you out a blessing.'" She went on, "That wasn't something for you to turn down or accept; God was proving to you he exists."

Now I had a firsthand experience showing me that spirits are close to me, and they are there to assist, to protect, and to guide. I learned we have only but to ask for what we need, then believe we will receive it. However, that reception is based on God's time, not **our** time. I continued my healing work with other spiritual teachers until one day, my guardian angel led me to a priestess. Although the religion she belongs to has many different names throughout the mostly Latin countries that practice it, in the United States it is known as Yoruba or, more commonly, *Santeria.*

That was the moment Ms. *Lulu came into my life. I worked with this beautiful Santera for about two years. She was about my height, a little over five feet tall, with a short bob and an inviting smile. There was a warmth to her energy, that made me feel safe and comfortable. I went to Ms. Lulu for tarot readings on my life, spiritual baths, counseling about college, and even boys.

Ms. Lulu was a constant in my life, and I had grown to love her as a second mother. Two years had passed, and I started dreaming about the *orishas,* the saints of the Santeria religion. Once I felt I had found a sense of balance again,

I decided—or maybe was even guided—to join the religion myself.

At the time, I thought becoming an initiate would lead me to a sense of belonging and acceptance. Remember I mentioned being the odd one in my family? I was a loner among my siblings, maybe because I was the middle child and rarely felt like a priority.

I also hoped joining the religion, would help me find direction and a new family dynamic absent the drama I was running away from in my biological family. So, I made an appointment with Ms. Lulu to start the initiation process, but then one day, she was gone. I no longer had a way to contact her, later finding out from members in her *ocha*^G family that she had moved to the West Coast. I was devastated I could no longer continue the process with her. Part of me felt betrayed she left without giving any notice or the opportunity to become familiar with someone else.

As a result, I went to someone Ms. Lulu was acquainted with in the religion, another priest she knew. He lived in the Bronx; I had seen him a few times in the *botanica*^G where she worked. He was her mother's godchild, and later became my *padrino* (godparent).

Standing eye length to me, he sported a triangular gray patch in the front of his hairline and a huge beer belly; his stomach always hung out over his clothes. When I first met him in the religious store I went for a tarot card reading, he seemed to have a calm demeanor. I quickly realized: looks can be deceiving.

The day my path to being initiated began, I sat in a dark basement in a small stand-alone two-story house up in the South Bronx. As I entered, there was a faint smell of burnt herbs—I thought was sage with a lingering scent of Florida water, both commonly used in Santeria. This was one of the first steps to joining the religion and I was overjoyed to have gotten through the initial phase. I then wore *los elekes*, small round colorful beads, hung on a string I wore around my neck.

Three elders put each *eleke* on, slowly, one by one, while they sang in the traditional Yoruba language. As they began to close the ceremony, I was given a brief explanation of the different rules and restrictions of each necklace, five in total. After I received the sacred protection beads, a period of self-reflection began. Just as there are many Catholic saints—too many to list here, there are many orishas. Each *eleke* I received represented a particular *santo* and their element.

For the purposes of this book, I write only about my relationship with my protecting saint Yemaya, the goddess of the ocean, motherhood, and fertility.

With my newfound AWAKENING, I began to process the ceremony I had just gone through. With that thought, I wanted and yearned to learn more.

Unknown to me, in Santeria, questions are not the correct way to start: you learn through observing and doing. I asked the priest— who was then my *padrino*—a question about a another initiate in the room. Unexpectedly, and to my surprise, the response I received was rude and the beginning of the verbal abuse I was to endure for three years. His response to my question was, *"THAT AIN'T NONE OF YOUR BUSINESS!"* And with that, he abruptly turned his back on me and walked away. I was disheartened, to say the least. I was new and eager to learn.

No one had explained to me the most basic principles of the religion. You don't ask—you watch, you observe, and that's how you learn. Over the following years, the subconscious motto for me and others was "I insult you —that's how you learn." I pushed the encounter to the back of my mind and brushed it off as "maybe he is just stressed and having a bad day." I decided to proceed and continue working with him.

Before the actual initiation, there are many stages, most of which I will not discuss here. One stage is attending a *misa,* or spiritual mass. During the process, we sit in a group, usually in a circular formation.

Several spirits will pass messages through mediums also in the prayer circle. As I was about to join the religion with another person, both she and I sat inside the circle. Right at the beginning, a hostile spirit came my way, channeled by my *padrino* at the time. He was a true psychic and a very experienced medium who helped me communicate with this deceased family member.

She confessed to all the spiritual negativity she had brought to me and other family members when she was on the earthly plane. She wanted to be released from the prison she was confined to because of her wicked past deeds; she was asking for forgiveness. I fought doing so, but eventually I did. Granting her request also released a generational curse that had followed me from the time I was born. I was getting a clean start in life—or so I thought.

On October 3, 1999, I was fully initiated into the religion as a Santeria priestess. Out of respect for the *santos* and those who still practice the religion, I cannot share specific details about the actual process.

However, I can tell you that the ceremony itself is like an eight-hour workday, but it really is a yearlong process. For me it was a time where I was able to really bond with and settle into my new life, the new world I had accepted —the world I had chosen.

Three days after the initiation ceremony was completed and without provocation, my *padrino* called me at home, *cursed* at me, and wrongly accused me of something I did not do. When I confronted him, his response was, "Well, what did you expect?" Santeria, a beautiful religion, has no formal book, no Sunday school to teach you how to behave or what questions are appropriate to ask or not to ask. You learn by participating and helping your godparents in ceremonies.

However, if that interaction is shrouded with verbal abuse, disrespect, and a lack of empathy for an initiate's feelings, it can ruin the experience. My learning became masked with resentment.

HEART LOCKER #1

People show you who they are up front.
Whether or not you choose to
see it is up to you.

I did my best to establish clear boundaries with my *padrino*. I wanted him to understand that cursing and shouting were triggers for me and not acceptable. However, this was territory I had before never crossed into. I had lived my whole life until then just "taking the abuse." That was normal behavior for me. And now, as a young lady, I was doing my best to change. It was fruitless, however; I was dealing with someone stuck in their own way of thinking. Attempting to draw a line in the sand with him became a waste of time. The verbal insults continued until one day I decided: enough. It was close to Oshun's day in September 2003. I knew this *santo* as the beautiful river orisha that governed love affairs and matters of the heart.

This was the period in my life I refer to as the AWAKENING. I was living in Canarsie, Brooklyn, at the time. It was the weekend, I believe. If you're a New Yorker, then you know on most weekends the trains run slower because of track work. Sometimes passengers must instead use shuttle buses or even cabs to get around. I left my home in the very early morning hours, excited to help my *ocha* family and my *padrino* set up the site for Oshun's tambor (a party for the santo).

I left home at about five thirty a.m. and arrived at the cultural center in Spanish Harlem around seven fifteen a.m.

At seven thirty, I was once again verbally assaulted by the priest who initiated me. There had been a series of incidents of disrespectful behavior he himself had endured, and I realized I had been used as a punching bag for his frustrations.

I was on my knees in front of the *santo* with my godsisters around me when he screamed into my face and turned his back on me. I had never encountered that kind of rage before. It was as though I had received the anger he had carried throughout his entire life, or perhaps many lifetimes. I felt severely verbally assaulted. That day was the last day I would ever consider him my godfather. Mentally, I left his *ocha* house, though physically I continued to play along as if nothing had happened. I forced a smile on my face, pretending to let the incident roll off my back. However, inside I was hurting. I had no real way to communicate how I was feeling. I did not know how to tell this person I no longer wanted to be his godchild and wanted him out of my life. I had made a mistake choosing him as a godparent.

I had lost the small modicum of respect I had left for him. In his all-female *ocha* house (with the exception of one male godchild) he seemed to enjoy making his goddaughters feel weak.

Then it became known over time that he had his own maternal issues, and in my opinion this was why he was unable to allow women to lead or be in their power.

I didn't know how to tell him the truth, and I did not have the courage to leave.

I would have a mental battle with myself. Some days I felt empowered: "I'm out of this house and done with this priest." Then other days I would ask myself, "Where would I go then ?" I went back and forth in my mind for months.

I spent the next year looking for another group, another family within the religion, with no luck. On every chance I saw an opportunity to leave, I would feel my guardian saint Yemaya would tell me, "*Not yet.*" I never understood why she advised me not to leave, considering the verbal abuse and disrespect she herself had witnessed. It wasn't until a decade later that it all became clear, about which I will go into more detail later in the book. At times, I had this feeling of being powerless and not healed enough to go on my own. Fortunately, the universe opened a door for me.

Over time, I found that my godparent was in too much emotional pain of his own to be of any real assistance to me. It was time for me to move on.

I had bought into the lies I was told as an initiate. There were moments I was led to believe if I ever left the group, I would have all kinds of problems and pitfalls in my life, "because the *santos* do not acknowledge the person who did not perform the initiation ceremony."

In my case, what the *padrino* said was not the truth. Once I chose to move on from the *ocha* house and the godparent who initiated me, I felt a sense of relief, as though a weight had lifted off my shoulders. But more on my exit later.

While looking for another person to work with, I started mentoring sessions with *Hector. I thank the universe for bringing him into my life. I started connecting with him in the fall of 2003.

He became my beloved life coach and confidant and for about a decade, I spoke to him for healing sessions, counseling, and support.

Hector taught me to ground and balance with the Earth's energy, a meditation exercise I will talk more about later. He also taught me to energetically break contracts and form healthy boundaries with myself and others. After I'd shared my past in detail, he helped me notice a behavioral pattern that had formed in my life.

I was in a repeating "karmic loop," as he explained. I learned karmic loops are situations with various individuals that played out repeatedly throughout our lives. It could appear with the same person as it does with a sibling or spouse, or it could play out with different people in different circumstances, such as with coworkers and distant relatives.

Hector, upon learning of the verbal assaults I endured the three active years I practiced Santeria, encouraged me to leave. However, I wasn't ready to take that leap just yet. I didn't have the faith or confidence to be on my own.

Eventually I moved out of state, relieved that I could use the distance as an excuse to stay away from the priest who initiated me. I would travel by bus or train to New York for infrequently cowrie shell readings with my *padrino*, the more common way to communicate with the *santos*. If he saw me twice a year, he was lucky. There was a time I would mark on my calendar a scheduled quarterly phone call, just to stay on "good terms" with him, in case I needed something done for the saints. My *padrino* was the type who, if you did not speak to him or give him attention (he had a Napoleon complex), then you would be overcharged when you did ask for his help. How did I know this?

I would compare what I had to pay for ceremonies or readings versus what my godsisters were charged. There were two incidents I remember when I paid more than I should have.

Still in the process of developing my ability to communicate with spirits, I had to rely on the priest who initiated me to communicate with the *santos*. Even though I knew I had a support system with my life coach Hector, he was not experienced in the ways of the religion.

I believed the mistruths about leaving and continued to stay a part of the *ocha* house, though I desperately wanted to leave. I remained on the outskirts of the group and did the bare minimum.

I would arrive late to events and leave early. I avoided the priest who initiated me at all costs and continued to focus on the new growth cycle I had started.

More blessings started coming my way, and more doors began to open. With a new job offer, I had a chance to train and study microbiology with some of the best in the field. I accepted the opportunity, and with my little backpack and two carry-on duffel bags, I hopped on a bus to Pennsylvania.

In November 2007, I began a new stage of my healing process. It was both a challenge and a reward working in Philadelphia. Grateful for the opportunity to start over, I continued the growth process while everything and everyone around me gradually changed.

It wasn't until I relocated that I realized negative thought patterns, when not addressed, will resurface no matter where you are. The location and circumstances of my life had changed, but the lessons were still unlearned and the issues unresolved.

HEART LOCKER #2

Your issues will follow you to
another city, state or planet.
Until they are healed.

facing the darkness

Hector was an intuitive and gifted healer. We worked together virtually through phone and email sessions for more than a decade. Although we never met in person, we had a true spiritual bond; we were soul mates. My definition of a "soul mate" is simple: I believe our souls knew each other from past lives. And yes, I believe I have lived in other lifetimes. But in this one, Hector was sent to help guide me back to *myself.* He taught me meditations to help me ground and feel more centered. This was the most important technique I learned and remains the most helpful. Grounding is a metaphysical technique of visualizing an energy cord from the base of your sacrum—your first *chakra*[G]—that extends all the way to the center of the earth (Diagram 1).

My journey into chakra healing started with Hector's guidance. Chakras are energy centers—or what I call "energy ports." While all chakras are vital, the most important at the initial time of my healing work was the root chakra. That was how I learned to keep myself grounded through periods of confusion, both internal and external. I will share more about the chakras and different energy centers later in my journey.

We worked on releasing traumas from both my past and my present. Some of the more difficult past experiences involved growing up in a dysfunctional home, but what family doesn't have their own issues? However, there were frequent patterns of behavior I felt were verbal abuse and many instances of disrespect. I'm sure there are family members who will not agree, and that's okay. It's a free country, and everyone has a right to their own opinion; I'm just sharing my experience.

The insults were always masked as "constructive criticism." I didn't realize how much damage words could really do to a child. To this day, at age forty-seven, I remember phrases from when I was in my early twenties that still upset me. "You're always in need of financial assistance"—what a nasty way to speak to someone. But the question remains, What was really behind those words? Was it concern, or was it just hitting below the belt? Was it meant to motive me? Or was it meant to spite me? This was the period I refer to as *FACING THE DARKNESS*.

My definition for "facing the darkness" is the same as confronting another part of me. It was the same as going so deep into my traumas, I began to see another side of myself. This side is that part of your spirit that needs to be healed. Again, everyone has their own path in life— their own sense of belonging, their own life lessons. I'm sharing what I have learned over the years and hopefully those lessons will help someone achieve enlightenment sooner rather than later.

It took two decades—roughly twenty-two years—for me to reach a sense of peace, to feel somewhat whole again. I have continued to learn and experience new aspects of myself; it's a lot easier than it used to be! I have the tools to create the life I want. I have the knowledge and guidance of my guardian angels. I'll share more about my journey to connecting with spirits in later chapters.

Diagram 1.

Coaching Session from 7/2005
The Art of Grounding

1. Visualize creating a
grounding cord from the
energy center near the base
of your spine to the center of
the Earth.

2. Imagine that cord as a
solid stream of light
connecting to the center of
the Earth.

3. Then allow the streams of
energy to drain from the
different chakras down to
Earth.

Earth

Facing my dark side with Hector was difficult at times. I wasn't always willing to be open to new information. Having experienced so many hardships and what I felt were setbacks, I became stuck in my ideas and what I thought was correct behavior.

I believed there was something wrong with everyone else and that I was always right. *There's nothing wrong with me. I'm not the problem. **They** are the problem. And I need to solve their problems—* then I can feel better about myself, I would think. However, that is not the truth. The problems that repeated were new opportunities for the soul, my soul, to learn.

Believe me, this was a very harsh reality to accept. To open my mind to a different way of thinking. To accept that I was responsible, that I had created all the problems in my life, all of my "self-created issues." The truth was, *I* was the problem—me.

When I was little, I would hear people would say "Sticks and stones will break my bones, but words will never hurt me." Well, I beg to differ. When you're a young woman trying your wings at independence, you remember the disrespect. You remember the nasty energy behind those words. You remember the lack of support. You remember the insults.

Grounding helped me release those words from my space, the negative memories I held on to. I also learned that words hold energy. Whether the words are positive (compliments and encouragement) or negative (insults and put-downs), they all hold an energetic frequency. The main objective is to focus on a state of equanimity—in other words, a state of neutrality.

I found once I achieved this state of peace—which always changes as you encounter highs and lows throughout life—it really didn't matter what anyone else's thoughts were, only my own. No one's opinion was going to pay my bills or put food on my table; therefore, why did I care? This was another beautiful epiphany I experienced on my ascension journey.

My life coach taught me how to meditate and imagine those hurtful words as seeds, big or small, and then visualize blowing them up. Sometimes we would combine meditation techniques, sending those seeds down my grounding cord.

Once I started on this spiritual path of growth, I realized the more memories I cleared, the more came up to be released and worked through. I had no idea how challenging walking a spiritual path could be. Once you begin, though, it's difficult stop. The feeling of healing is addictive, to say the least.

I became obsessed with it, always keeping in mind the objective to one day be free of my godfather and his group. Over time, I became keenly aware my growth would determine whether I stayed or moved on from this organization. With that thought in mind, I continued the ascension process. Eventually, all that inner work led me to the reality of karmic debts.

Those are the experiences where I was hurt or hurt someone and now, I must do repair work and break the cycle. Hector referred to this concept as another example of a karmic loop. After I made the decision to distance myself from my *padrino*, I continued to engage in meditations for clearing away past painful experiences. What I found was that holding on to those painful memories can manifest as physical pain. For example, sometimes when I recalled an unkind word said to me in the past, I would feel pain in my stomach or a tightness in my chest.

Hector taught me pain held in the gut area could also cause internal imbalances; unsurprisingly, I was suffering from severe bloating, constipation, and other forms of intestinal imbalances. I am sharing my experiences with the hope of someone benefitting from them. There are so many religious models that exist in the world, and I hold no judgment against any of them. If a prayer or chant helps your growth process, great! We are here on earth as a learning experience for the soul. And this is the wonderful, beautiful world of choice.

Living in Philly, there were days I wondered, *Is this a test of faith from the universe or an opportunity for a brand-new start at life?* I wasn't sure my move was the right decision; I was trusting my intuition.

Before I moved to Pennsylvania, I wrote to various clinical researchers asking if there were any open positions in their labs. Fortunately, in November 2007, someone replied. Was it divine inspiration? I like to think so. I believe, to this day, that I was guided to make that change. I never felt alone; I knew my guardian angels were there with me every step of the way. Even when I doubted my decision, I went through with the changes.

Trials and problems kept repeating, and at some point, I had another epiphany. The difficulties I had with other people were just opportunities to heal myself. At the time, I didn't see things that way. I felt I was under attack and was often used as a punching bag for other people's frustrations. I hadn't yet realized I had unknowingly created those situations to help me change.

Healing sessions with Hector also coupled as mentoring sessions. He came into my life and encouraged me to take the focus off the godparent and family members I was dealing with and put the focus and attention toward myself.

My life coach continued to encourage me to leave the *ocha* house, but my soul wasn't ready. Not only was it not ready, but my guardian saint, Yemaya, continued to discourage making any changes. At the time, my communication with my spirit guides was not clear and there were many blocks due to the intense amount of healing work required.

As time went on and I continued working with Hector, my connection to the spirit and to my inner knowing became clear and distinct. I could feel the saint telling me "No." However, it was not a *"No, you can never leave"*; it felt more like *"It's not the right time."* The saint is always there to guide me through life. Even though I was itching to leave, I also felt leaving without the saint's permission might cause unforeseen problems.

HEART LOCKER #3

Other people's annoying behavior is usually an exaggerated version of your OWN.

pay your dues

My training as a medical technologist began at a hospital in Pennsylvania, in spring of 2008. Before that I was working in a research laboratory within the same institution. However, like many research positions, when the study ends, so does the position. I was grateful to transition into another job, that same month.

Initially, I had mixed feelings, moving from a clinical laboratory in New York City to a facility in a different state. I thought it would have been an easy transition, considering I had worked in clinical research most of my life. At times, it was like a juggling act: I was adjusting to life in a new environment, working with multiple defined procedures and thousands of patient specimens every month, as well as pursuing my continued growth and healing exercises. The training was difficult, because of all the different regulations. There were many standard operating procedures (SOPs) for every type of specimen and manually processing them was also very complicated. Let's not forget the different policies for sending and receiving results from off-site reference laboratories. I won't even go into the steps and red tape that existed when there was an "out-of-range" critical result.

"Whew—*Me duele la cabeza!*" I would joke with my Spanish friends: I have a pain in my head. Finally, I caught on, but it took months. I eventually found it was not the workload that was the true challenge. It wasn't even the multitude of rules, regulations, and SOPs that had to be adhered to. The true challenge was navigating the landmine of personalities and spiritual testing I was about to endure. I guess that was what many would term PAYING YOUR DUES.

Her personality, my personality, their personalities; it's all *mishigas*^{G}. I found myself attempting to pilot among different kinds of people, from the most difficult to the easiest. However, the interesting part was every person, every coworker I encountered at this new job, seemed to be a mirrored image of some aspect of my own personality. While that was very true, determining what parts of me needed to change was not easy.

One of the individuals who was the most challenging to deal with and triggered me the most was a technologist in a senior level position with whom I started to work. I gave him the nickname "Bat Shit Crazy," but here I call him *Arthur. He was assigned to train me when I was hired, and it wasn't long until our energies started to clash. It started with verbal abuse that eventually led to physical abuse on his part and ultimately a complaint being filed with upper-level management, on my part.

At first, everything was good. I tried to pick up the proper techniques for specimen handling and processing, but there were so many rules to master. Compounding the difficulty was working with someone who had abuse issues of his own and had not addressed them. I have found I always encountered people who had a set of carry-on luggage, or in simple terms, had their own issues or healing work to do.

The difficult part is dealing with someone not willing to look at their own "darkness." I had the motivation to go to the source of my problems, address them, and correct them. Clearly, that was not the case with Arthur.

Working as a technologist was not something I had formally trained for; I learned in the field. Now, I had some prior experience working with laboratory guidelines, but never so many. A super heavy workload and a harassing coworker do not make for a comfortable working environment. I made every attempt to apply the rules I had learned with the *padrino* I was separated from.

My motto was "Keep my distance—heal myself." I set out with the idea to create an invisible line between me and the personality that never seemed to let up. Throughout all of 2009 were sporadic incidents of verbal abuse and insults thrown my way.

Those assaults began to escalate; eventually the name-calling followed. While I was working, I was referred to as a "fool" and told to "get the hell out of that chair" in front of my coworkers.

Trying to find some harmony with Arthur, I once asked him why he was so unkind to me. His response: "Because you act like your shoe size." As time passed, I tried to establish healthy boundaries, hoping Arthur would focus on his own healing instead of using me as an avoidance tactic.

HEART LOCKER #4

There are no victims only volunteers.
People treat you the way you
ALLOW them to treat you.

Weekly sessions with my life coach were very much needed at that time. I was in a completely new environment attempting to find a happy balance. Away from the family, friends, and life I had known in New York City for thirty-plus years, I felt like I was starting over. The transition became easier when Hector and I focused on grounding exercises that cleared my space of negative energy. Feelings of uncertainty—did I make the right decision with this move?—also started to go away. Then he introduced me to a meditation exercise called "breaking contracts."

This type of meditation allows you to mentally imagine you have a contract with someone, then set the intention to dissolve or burn it. What this does is release any energetic bonds between you and that other person. It is an energetic "divorce" of sorts.

Coaching Session from 7/2008

Breaking Contracts

Visualize a sheet of paper on your mental screen. Then repeat "My intent is to now remove, release, and unbind any and all other spiritual and other contracts between myself and _____ (the name of the person) which no longer serve our highest good and the highest good and welfare of all creation right now and so it is".

I then allowed myself to imagine a contract set on fire and burning, then disappearing. As the contract burns, so does my connection to that person and any *karma/karmic*^G debts that are owed. Now this type of meditation does help, and it will take the edge off a tense encounter with someone you're dealing with. However, it may need to be repeated until you have learned the lesson or changed the aspect of your personality that needs to be healed—that part of your personality that is a mirror image to the other person.

The technique worked, and Arthur did back off. However, the verbal abuse would soon begin again. I used the technique frequently, maybe once a month, from the spring to the fall of 2009. Consistently repeating the meditation was necessary until that karmic debt was over.

February 2010 was the turning point for me, in that situation. Sticks and stones—I can ignore most insults, but when the words turn into physical contact, that's stepping into a new territory, a space I'm not willing to accept.

At last, my moment of change had come. Through meditation, I started putting the pieces together and asking myself the questions we all don't like to ask. "Was this difficult scenario actually a self-created situation?"

In the past, the old Niomi would point fingers and say, "It's them—they have the problem!" The truth was, I was the person who needed to change.

After meeting with upper-level management about my formal harassment complaint, I was nervous about the outcome and any possible retaliation. However, I felt relieved I no longer had to silently battle this person on my own. Relieved I no longer had to suffer in silence. Relieved I no longer had to carry this weight on my shoulders. After a year of escalating verbal assaults, name-calling, and degrading behavior, I got the lesson. Every difficult life experience, for me, is always followed by a lesson, an epiphany. My "a-ha!" moment, my "I got it!" moment, the time it just all made sense, finally arrived.

I was home meditating and that little inner voice asked: *Why are you taking this abuse? Do you want to continue to be a victim your whole life?* And with that thought, I planned a method of change. It all started to become clear. I was in a repetitive pattern. As a child, growing up in a home with what I felt was "justified" abusive behavior, it became normal for someone to insult me. Children do not get to choose the types of energy surrounding them. For adults, it was different.

Now, finally, I accepted the universe's invitation to choose. "Stay in this victim frequency and continue to be live bait for abusers or make the changes necessary to move on from this toxic dynamic," it seemed to say to me.

It became obvious why this person was in my life and why it was necessary for me to break contracts with him. WE WERE MATCHING FREQUENCIES!

I couldn't believe it. I just could not accept that I had created this painful reality due to my own ignorance. Because I continued to see myself as a victim, that low vibration established a frequency to attract low-vibration abusers. Arthur and I were matching frequencies. I the victim and he the abuser. It was time for me to raise my frequency and exit left this karmic dynamic. This cat-and-mouse game of "you abuse me, I accept the abuse" was over. And with that thought, the lesson was done.

The inclusion of my supervisors and other high-level administrators did put an end to Arthur's verbal assaults and physically threatening behavior. When I filed the complaint with management, Arthur was reprimanded, which relieved some of the pressure. His bad behavior, however, continued, albeit in more subtle ways, because he was not engaged in his own inner work. But, poof, be gone! He had no more power. I continued to focus on my work and my healing, while he began to make complaints against me.

These subtle forms of retaliation fell on deaf ears. Every false report he submitted against me, was met with resistance from management.

To my fortune, Arthur and I were no longer frequency matches. I raised my energetic vibration by healing my feelings as a victim. He continued to stay in that low abusive frequency, but his behavior no longer had an effect. Mentally I had moved on from the situation.

He resigned a few months later.

HEART LOCKER #5

Lessons will usually come in stages.
First a whisper, then a brick, then a bat.
The experience becomes more
severe until its mastered.

choose you

Since the fall of 2010, I have always envisioned my birthday month as the time for self-reflection. Not just on myself, but more on what lessons the universe taught me, how much I had grown and the fact I had just overcome one of the most difficult periods of my life. Extreme verbal abuse and the beginnings of physical abuse were behaviors I'd never had to deal with on a job. My only experience dealing with such strong personalities had been in my own family.

Being the middle child, sometimes I could easily get lost in the crowd. I came from a family with a strict West Indian heritage and many times, I felt I was not always seen as a person. There was so much controlling behavior, I often believed my siblings and I were not allowed to have our own voices. In most cases, "This is the way it is" was what we were told.

I saw an escape from constant control and what I believed was a lack of respect for my boundaries. When the opportunity arrived for me to go away to college, I jumped at the chance to move. For me it really was a chance to finally be on my own, one of those times when you must CHOOSE YOU.

I used my birthday month—I'm a November baby—to look back on 2009 and the extreme harassment I had suffered. You never know how strong you are until you must be. That was the most complicated lesson the universe brought my way, and I survived because I focused on my healing and not on the behavior of my abuser.

What I have discovered is a person's behavior reflects how they see themselves.

An abused person will most likely abuse others, and a harasser has most likely been harassed themselves. I chose to not repeat the patterns, to work on myself and my awakening to a better, healthier way of life.

Before I focused on my spiritual growth, my words could be harsh when I spoke; that has since changed. My behavior could also be seen as abusive, such as asking a friend to do something that made them uncomfortable.

For example, guilt-tripping a friend to let me use their cell phone to call an ex and hang up. You know what I mean—after a breakup you just need to hear the other person's voice, but not really speak to them. My friends wanted to stay out of the drama, and I knew that, but I would ask them for help. Now I'm more aware of my own behavior and how I treat people.

Arthur was a huge, exaggerated version of my problems that needed to be healed. When he resigned, the harassment ended; however, the universe continued to bring other coworkers into my life with matching frequencies and mirrored personalities traits. Although it was difficult to control my sarcasm at times, that aspect became more noticeable whenever someone gave me a taste of my own attitude.

New hires came in with their own issues and back-talking tendencies. I thought I was the Queen of Comebacks until I had one smart aleck after another to deal with. Kudos to the universe for bringing the right people around me and creating the opportunity to learn, to heal, and to ascend.

I continued to focus on my past childhood traumas with my life coach. Then, one day, I had this strange feeling. *I just don't want to be anyone's godchild anymore.*

When I decided to leave Santeria, it was no easy task. But now, fifteen years later, I was in a calm position in my life and I had clear thoughts. There was no more doubt about what I had learned and the next steps in my growth cycle. Finally, my guardian saint, Yemaya, gave me permission to leave. I was given the green light to move on—from both my godparent and the religion completely.

Don't mistake what I've written; Santeria is a beautiful religion. There were many wonderful moments and interacting directly with the saints was awesome, especially when given the opportunity to speak to them on the third dimensional earthly plane. They are high-vibrational beings and it is a blessing to have them in my life.

A person's behavior is separate from the religion. Although the group I worked with did help me in finding my way out of the darkness, my *padrino's* behavior made me feel uncomfortable. Continuing in his group would have been counterproductive to my spiritual development. I have no problems working or learning with someone who has their own healing work to do. However, I cannot continue to be in the presence of anyone who, on a personal level, is not willing to make the necessary changes for their own spiritual growth. I can only focus on my own healing. If someone chooses to live their life in pain, that is their choice. I will never again allow myself to be a receptacle for someone avoiding their own problems.

When a person is hurt, they will most likely hurt others and this has been my experience. I had suffered verbal abuse from the priest who initiated me too many times —lesson learned.

My choice to leave Santeria had nothing to do with the religion. I left because of the behavior of the godparent. I left because of the way I was treated. I left because of the way I *allowed* myself to be treated. I saw no progress in the other person and no culpability for his behavior. We were no longer a frequency match, and again, this relationship came to an end.

HEART LOCKER #6

Hurt people
HURT people

I released my saints gently and respectfully back into their elements. I overcame the fear of leaving the group and being on my own, because I had done the healing work and cleared the blockages between me and the *orishas*. No longer was there a need for a godparent to act as a third party; I could now speak to the *santos* directly.

In all fairness, the godparent I dealt with at one point said, "I took the obligation off; you don't need to come around anymore." Although I appreciated that, if I hadn't been fed so many lies, I would have left sooner.

I wanted to go but was advised by my *santo*, "Not yet." Now I understand that my spiritual contract with him was not over at the time. I believe the *padrino* knew there was damage to our relationship beyond repair and that he was the cause. It was only a matter of time before I moved on and he tried to push me out of his group. Similar to the Arthur experience, I had spiritually ascended and was no longer a frequency match to the *padrino*. As a result, one attempted to force me out of a job, the other wanted me out of his *ocha* house. And then, the time came.

I had finally freed myself of the shackles of that victim mentality, that powerless way of thinking. I had taken back control of my life.

I can honestly say it was one of the happiest days of my life when my contract with the *padrino* came to an end. I no longer had to continue dealing with someone choosing to live their life in pain. And with the permission of Yemaya, I left Santeria in March of 2014.

With that experience behind me, I continued working with my life coach, Hector. I looked forward to what the future would bring now that I was free of any restrictions from the group. With a new outlook on life and a better idea of where I wanted to go, I started to keep a journal. Although I had on occasion kept a small diary at the start of my awakening, I wasn't consistent with it.

During the process of growth and ascension, it was a challenge for me to stay focused on my day-to-day activities. I didn't think much or do much outside of work other than focus on meditation, energy healing, and improving my health. Because I was not in alignment with God's plan for my life, every part of it was affected. My healing was a mountain that I was still in the process of climbing. In the past, food and overeating was my escape from past traumas. I knew I needed to find a healthier way of dealing with my issues.

Food had been my best friend since forever. At five foot two, there was a time I weighed almost three hundred pounds. I've since shed a lot of the extra weight.

Truly, that's what I saw my extra rolls as: unresolved baggage. The more I healed myself and the more I ascended, the less I saw food as something to abuse.

I ate when I wasn't hungry; I just needed to fill that emptiness I felt inside of myself. There is no shame in sharing this part of my growth cycle. I think on some level, most people have a way of coping with a difficult time in their lives. For me, it was food. For others, it may be alcohol, drugs, or even gambling.

In my opinion, nothing is wrong with any of those; it's the excess that's the problem. It's when the activity is abused and becomes an addiction, other aspects of our lives start to deteriorate because we lose control.

My health suffered because I couldn't stop eating. Others suffer when gambling or alcohol becomes an addiction. You can end up in debt with uncontrolled gambling or liver damage with uncontrolled drinking.

I've seen the effects of addiction firsthand through friends, acquaintances, and even former energy healers I've worked with. The meditations helped me to start loving myself enough to stop harming my body with food.

Once I healed that victim way of thinking and started to live a more empowered life, my external appearance gradually began to reflect the internal change I was going through. I was becoming healthy, inside and out.

I discovered my healing had taken different forms during my growth periods. Once I'd learned a lesson or experience, a new one would come along.

It might not be as challenging, though, because now I had the tools to handle them in a better way. Removing toxicity from my life also meant clearing the negativity which had caused confusion and doubt in my inner knowing at the beginning of this journey.

As I worked with my life coach, undergoing constant meditation, the truth began to reveal itself. Finally, the day arrived when the universe revealed what had been done to me in the early 1990s—that time when I was confused and felt lost with no sense of direction. I'd had my suspicions but no concrete proof. My instincts told me one thing while my ego said "NO!" Would a family member be so brazen, so bold, as to throw negative energy my way?

Would a family member be so weak they would feel the need to control and deliberately attempt to block my inner knowing, forcing me to stay in a dependent state for years?

Could this be the reason I lost my edge?

Some people do believe in hexes—I'm one of them. As I said before, there is good and bad in most situations. And harm can be done in many ways. I don't want to discuss or give specific examples of the spell work that was done to me. No one should ever engage in those kinds of destructive acts. Sending negativity and doing spiritual work to hurt someone comes with a *price*. You get back what you put out in life!

Yes, I do believe a family member put a curse on me, or what is informally referred to in Santeria as a *trabajo*[G]. Do I have proof ? No, not in the three-dimensional physical plane. However, in the spiritual realm, the evidence is overwhelming, and that's where everything became clear.

I started to reflect back to the period when I struggled to keep my focus, my direction in life, my sanity. Yes, it all began when I left for college when I was just nineteen years old. This "fight" continued for the next twenty-plus years of my life. Once I realized what was done, then came the *journey* to recover from it. Even with family, you can have some relatives who are supportive and others willing to do what they thought was justified harm.

This relative is still on the earthly plane and one day will have to answer for what *los santos* deemed as "*profound disrespect.*" I never retaliated; I refused to take from God the right to vindicate me. I will just leave this part of the story as—to be continued.

I was able to finally move on from that difficult time in my life that made any progress challenging. Really and truly, no one's dark energy can affect you unless you allow it to.

However, that energy is just that: energy. And for someone like me at that time, unaware of how to transmute negativity, that lack of knowledge in protecting myself caused my progress in life to be a struggle. I continued to move forward in life and achieve, gaining undergraduate and graduate degrees. However, I struggled through work, through school and failed romances. Every aspect of my life was affected.

Slowly, I was putting the pieces back together with the help of the *santos,* energy healers, spirit guides, and lots of prayer. My guardian saint, Yemaya, and all the *orishas* were there to protect me. Even though I decided to leave the religion, they remained at my side, protecting and guiding me.

All I had to do was ask for assistance through prayer. As my grandfather once said, "Nothing comes without praying."

As I approached the end of this dark cycle, there was another pivotal change. Not all soul contracts are difficult or painful. Some spiritual contracts are benevolent and loving, as was the one I had with Hector.

It was an unusual feeling when we stopped working together. When our soul contract came to an end, it was bittersweet. I was grateful he came into my life and taught me many techniques to not only heal myself, but to learn to protect my energy as well. I will always remember him as that wonderful, bubbly life coach, who came into my life at just the right time.

Have you ever heard that saying, "When God closes a door, he opens a window"? It was so true. Spring of 2014 was a period of rapid changes for me. Multiple soul contracts ended as new ones began. The cycle of verbal abuse and manipulation was over. I had walked out of the darkness and into the *light*.

I can only focus on my own healing.

—NIOMI

Part Two

~∞~

INTO THE LIGHT

working with spirits

Dr. Lynn was such an elegant and caring teacher. Formally educated with a doctoral degree, she was also a highly intuitive and a gifted energy healer.

We started working together the same month my life coach decided to close his business and no longer take clients. When that happened, I panicked. Who would guide me through my healing process? Who would I depend on to call in the late hours for emergency healings when the pain became unbearable or when I went through moments of intense depression? Then the dark cloud started to lift, as I consciously began walking back into the light. Although there had been obstacles, I was still able to see through the depression, steering my life back to a balance and purpose again. Dr. Lynn helped me continue the growth process that has now given me the courage to share my path to enlightenment.

I continued to address past childhood traumas and those inflicted by my *padrino*. From this point on, I will just refer to him as "the priest from the religion." I am no one's godchild and will no longer use that term. The healing process felt like a test of commitment to my spiritual growth.

What I learned from that fifteen-year period as a Santera was not to join a religion or organization thinking it will solve all your problems. Chances are the opposite will happen, and you may end up dealing with someone with more issues than you have or feeling like you were disempowered. Fixing my own problems started with accepting the blame for the right choices as well as the wrong choices I made.

Remember, if you are not willing to accept culpability for the battles you are currently experiencing, don't expect anyone else to accept culpability for theirs.

I needed to believe I had the power to create the life I wanted and also to end all the conflicts.

Living in Philly, "the City of Brotherly Love," was amazing. Moving into a new phase of energy healing with a new mentor, I consciously chose to be around like-minded people, who also wanted to improve themselves.

This new path of healing now included developing my intuition, trusting my connection to the source, and harnessing my energy to function as a shield of protection. What I mean by that is using my *aura* ^{G} to discard negativity picked up from other people and then release it from any of my *chakra* ^{G} centers.

One of my spirit guides showed me a very specific meditation. (Some people use the terms guardian angel, ancestors, or even god's little helpers, whatever they are comfortable saying. "Spirits" and "my spirit guides" are my personal favorites.) As I stepped into a new phase of this ascension process, I encountered new helpers from the spirit world. You know, that place our souls go when we pass away and leave our physical bodies.

Dr. Lynn, using her channeling abilities, helped me communicate with one of the spirits who guided me. In one of her past lives, Ms. Hilda was a Romani dancer who taught me to find a happy place in my life.

As I was coming out of such an intense healing cycle, Ms. Hilda taught me different ways to protect my energy. Some of you may not believe we have lived in other ages or had past lives. I, however, choose to believe that I *have*. My spirit guide explained to me that, in one of her past lives, when she was a Sufi dancer, she used the process of "vortexing," or the ability to stand in your vortex (Diagram 2).

This process is a type of meditation where you visualize your energy spinning in the shape of a hurricane while anything you *don't* want within your space is pulled out and discarded down your grounding cord, to the center of the earth.

Diagram 2.

Mentoring Session 3/2014
SUFI DANCER – Spinning Vortex Meditation^{tm}

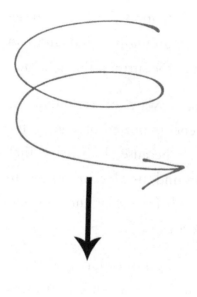

EARTH

1. Create a strong grounding cord to the center of the Earth.

2. Then visualize spinning anything you don't want in your energy field, in a circle and then down your grounding cord.

Spinning your vortex allows you to clean your energy field of other people's—and even your own—thoughts and vibrations. It allows you to be in a state of manifestation, to clear blocked energy and help you to create a happy life.

Another common technique is creating a protection rose. This type of meditation allows you to detox your energy space, maintain grounding, and, most importantly, give an evaluation of the surrounding energies (Diagram 3).

There are many ways or techniques one can use to preserve an energy vortex or energy field. I prefer the term "vortex" because I believe that energy flows constantly around us. It's up to us to maintain our energy at a high frequency and not allow anyone else's energy to affect us.

The beauty of the protection rose is it acts almost as a heads-up. It will tell you what your internal and external environments are like or what the "temperature" is, almost like a spiritual thermometer, a forewarning.

When the external world starts to get too "hot" or you feel overwhelmed with negative energy, the color and texture of the rose changes. For example, in that occasion the protection rose turns black and wilts.

My mentor explained that will occur when you're under psychic attack. When that happened to me, I knew additional techniques were necessary to clear my energy field and protect myself.

Usually, I would visualize my protection rose as a gold color. I would periodically check in, and most times the rose stayed unchanged. If there was no change in the color or texture of the rose, I knew my energy vortex was intact and my internal environment protected.

Not only did I see my protection rose as an added armor, but I also used it to remove and block negative energy being sent from another person.

Diagram 3.

Mentoring Session from 5/2014
Creating a Protection Rose

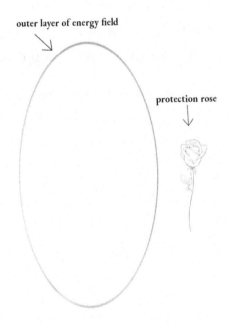

outer layer of energy field

protection rose

1. Create a strong grounding cord to the center of the Earth.

2. Create a rose on the external edge of your energy field.

3. Check periodically the freshness, color and quality of the rose.

4. If the rose wilts and becomes dark, you are on the receiving end of unwanted energy coming from outside your space.

5. Your protection rose has absorbed that energy.

6. Dissolve that rose, create a fresh one and make a mental note to check it more frequently.

For example, if my coworker arrived at work upset or angry, that created an unpleasant energy around me, and I would then mentally visualize myself creating and exploding roses. That meditation cleared the energy between us. I learned quickly to be aware of my thoughts and vibrations.

The protection rose was an added layer of security, helping to keep me in a high-vibrational frequency, protect my energy field, and maintain that internal vortex of energy.

When I went through different stages of a growth cycle, Ms. Hilda stressed the importance of keeping my mind balanced. I would sometimes have a difficult time staying focused, and my thoughts would wander. That again highlights the need of having an energy cord to the center of the earth. Being grounded helped to stabilize my thought process and focus on present-day experiences, rather than thinking about the past or the future. My mentor would say to stay in the *now*.

In the past, I would "lose my energy," and I had to learn to listen without absorbing another person's trauma. The most important lesson I learned from Ms. Hilda was to use my energy for myself before I shared it with someone else.

If I am not in a position of strength and balance, then I'm not helpful to anyone else. The most significant factor about the protection rose was that it was more effective when I removed the negative thoughts I had inside of me and the negative energy held in others.

Whenever I held on to a difficult scenario, I felt drained, as though I was stepping out of my vortex and creating a block. I quickly learned to preserve my thoughts for what I wanted to create in my life. Negativity and negative thoughts create energy blocks and stop you from attaining having what you desire.

I started to document my thoughts and feelings and gradually noticed those periods when I felt tired and depressed were usually during periods I had lost my grounding cord. Obsessing about how poorly someone treated me led to serious problems like uncontrolled outbursts.

At one time, I was the best at holding grudges—until I realized I was only hurting my mental and physical health. The best way to WORK WITH SPIRITS was to watch my *mouth*. My words, especially my TONE when I spoke to people, have done the most damage.

That was and has always been my biggest problem. I needed to say what I needed to say, in a loving way, release the thought, and move on.

The art of letting go—I'm still working on it! Ms. Hilda taught me the mind creates thoughts, the mouth expels words, and both hold energy.

There were times I would ask her why it seemed as though everything in my life was such a struggle. When we started working together, I was in a dream state. She showed me a healing symbol that looked like a scarecrow. I remember it as friendly and in the middle of a corn field. That same symbol came up in one of my healing sessions.

The only difference was that now the scarecrow had disappeared, and I saw the cornfield turn from rough to refined crystals. I asked her, "Why has this journey been so difficult for me? Why have the last fifteen years been tough lessons, tough lessons, and more tough lessons?" Her response came in the form of a parable. She showed me the image of a quartz crystal, a small one you could hold between your fingers. A bright little crystal. She said:

> " Think of the lessons as grains of sand that polish the crystal, and you are the crystal. A crystal can be polished with sand and made to be really beautiful. Sometimes, it can take years and years and years and years and years.

You have been polishing your crystal. This whole karmic pattern goes back to many lifetimes, the whole time you have been polishing your crystal. Now, you have a beautiful, bright crystal. It wouldn't be so beautiful and bright if it were not for all the grains of sand you encountered in your life."

And with that, I never saw Ms. Hilda again.

I found myself at the beginning of a new cycle of transformation, a new experience, accountability! I had just completed a long-standing healing project, that spanned many years. As I continued the new growth cycle, I also encountered different spirit guides. Ms.Hilda was the lovely guide that taught me about energy preservation and creating a joyful life. Along the way, there were other helpers who came into my life and started working with me.

This was an example of like attracts like. I had soul contracts with these guides. If the spirits and I had a matching experience, we would work together until it was time for us *both* to transition into a new lesson.

With a warm heart—no pun intended—I introduce to you Dr. Reginald Albright. And he absolutely was ALL BRIGHT. He came in with this intense, bright, and loving healing energy. In his time on the earthly plane, he was a heart surgeon. We had a soul contract that manifested when I began to develop heart issues. My doctor picked up on a developing slight murmur within the chambers of my heart and sent me to a cardiologist for additional testing. This was the point at which I really started to delve into the different chakras, or what I termed "energy ports." I read about each one and how they influenced a specific area of the physical body. (Diagram 4) gives a basic layout of the seven main chakras.

My healing work centered primarily around the second, third and fourth chakras. The fourth chakra is most related to the heart. And with Dr. Albright's keen attention to detail, he left no stone unturned and helped me to avoid a potential major illness.

What I learned through WORKING WITH SPIRITS was that an illness first manifests on the spiritual plane, then becomes real on the physical plane. When I write about the illness or disease forming, I mean it stems from your thoughts and experiences.

I'm talking about judgment, grudges, hostility, hate, anger—the list goes on. As I wrote before, energy can be used in the positive as well as the negative. And negative energy must either be dispelled or cleared away. When those thoughts go unchecked and are allowed to stay there, then we can get *problemas*.

In my case, I was on the precipice of a serious heart condition because I was holding onto negative experiences and past traumas. In previous chapters, I wrote about techniques to transmute energy. Whether it was using the Spinning Vortex Meditation™, grounding exercises, or visualizing the protection roses to clear my aura, my point is that I had control over my mind and what I *chose* to create on the external plane. If I wanted to stop this problem from becoming a heart disease, I had to change my diet and lose weight. But the most damage was being done by my thoughts. This was the wonderful way of the universe giving me an example of how powerful my mind is.

Through several sessions with my energy healer, Dr. Albright and his team helped energetically remove negative frequencies that had been forming around my heart. I had layers and layers of stored pain from past childhood wounds.

I can say I felt the effects shortly after, when it became easier for me to inhale and exhale. From the spirit world, Dr. Albright symbolically removed layers of fat from around my heart, and then it was my turn to do the work.

As a pescatarian now, I mostly eat seafood, fruits, and veggies. I still have a sweet tooth, and I indulge in the occasional *tres leches*, funfetti *flanchoco*, and my all-time favorite: *vigilantes* (Argentine croissants with custard and quince). I'm dreaming about some of them as I write this. Maybe I will take a train ride to the bakery in Union, New Jersey, and treat myself to some!

Really, we all have foods we like to indulge in, and that's okay. The problems lie in the excess. Once I began to change my diet to eating healthier foods and avoiding most, but not all, fried foods, then I started to become more active.

I used to hate exercise, but over time I looked forward to it. I joined a gym with a low monthly fee of $10 a month. As a night worker going straight to the gym after work at six thirty a.m., I could only manage ten or fifteen minutes of moderate walking on the treadmill. I gradually worked my way up to thirty minutes, then added soft cardio and weight training. The pinnacle of exercises for me was the stair climber. Ugh—every time I went into the gym, I would stare at those machines from across the room. In my mind I would say, "*Someday in the future, I'll get there*".

I'm still working on getting there as I write this book, ha ha ha!

Seriously, Dr. Albright did his part. He cleaned up and removed the negative energy pooled around my heart. He gave me a jump start, and now I had to maintain the

NIOMI NICCI

clearing. It was easy to change my diet and be more active. It was difficult to do the spiritual work to ensure I was never in that position again.

That meant doing the healing work on the inside to maintain a healthy mental environment. That's where chakra clearings become very important. At least for me, clearing my energy ports has been the most important work I have done to this day. Included is a very basic diagram and description of each energy port.

DIAGRAM 4 - THE 7 MAIN CHAKRAS

7. crown – in your head
6. forehead – some call this the third eye area
5. throat – pretty much what comes out of your mouth
4. chest area – mostly related to the heart, what we feel
3. stomach – when we feel things in our gut, the power center
2. pelvic – near the reproductive organs
1. gluteus/near the base of the spine – that's where the main grounding will occur.

78

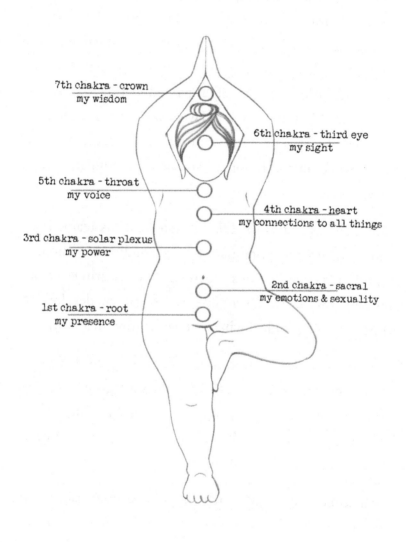

7th chakra - crown
my wisdom

6th chakra - third eye
my sight

5th chakra - throat
my voice

4th chakra - heart
my connections to all things

3rd chakra - solar plexus
my power

2nd chakra - sacral
my emotions & sexuality

1st chakra - root
my presence

Most of the healing work done in the fourth chakra focused on the chest pains and shortness of breath I suffered from. At first, I thought it was related to my weight, as I've always been plus-sized. I had gained a few pounds at that point, and I was attributing that shortness of breath to the recent weight gained. All the chakras are important, but, as so many layers were rapidly releasing, I believed it was better to start with one energy port and then work on the lessons that came up from the others gradually.

With the assistance of Dr. Albright and his team, I was saved from a potential heart condition. Then, I continued meditations focused on clearing energy around my heart. Over time as I began to develop my intuition, I could feel when energy became stagnant.

Occasionally in the morning, there was this feeling of bricks on top of my chest. I would start grounding and clearing energy from my heart chakra and I could feel the blockages dissipating. *Was it bloating?* Could have been, but the meditation did help.

Sometimes, even having regrets in life caused pain in my heart area. I had regrets about life choices, career choices, family choices and the list goes on. Thinking about what I could have done differently caused intense pain and made it difficult for me to breathe.

To be on the safe side, I followed up with a different cardiologist and had a barrage of blood tests done to make sure I was in a safe place and there was no more heart murmur. I needed to be sure I was in good health, and thankfully, I was. My blood tests came back normal with the exception of low potassium, which was due to one of the two medications I was taking. I was diagnosed with high blood pressure when I was twenty. My mom thinks I was showing signs at seventeen years old, but I dismissed the headaches back then, because I thought they were a possible side effect of just eating too many potato chips.

However, once I reached twenty, I started to feel sharp pains at the back of my neck. One day, a friend took my blood pressure while we were going through laboratory rotations for one of our classes and it was HIGH. And I mean *super* high—high enough to send me to the emergency room. Now, at forty-seven, my blood pressure is controlled. I continue to live on two antihypertensive medications and avoid most processed and fast foods.

Not to say I don't ever have those; I do love the fish sandwiches from a particular fast-food chain we all know.

I just don't have them for breakfast, lunch, and dinner anymore. Maybe I'll have a filet as a treat once or twice a month. Or even better, I'll make my own fish filets, which are just as good or sometimes even better!

A very prevalent form of energy I found that caused emotional pain was the "could haves," "should haves," and "would haves" in my life. They all created low vibration that would pool in my heart chakra. To manage my regret, I had to forgive myself. I had to forgive the idea that things could have been different.

That, for me, is the same as forgiveness. Forgiveness is not forgetting what the other person did or what I did or did not do; it is letting go of the idea of something different. Just accepting what was, what *is*, and planning out a path to start moving forward.

This remorse, this energy, was transmuted primarily by way of grounding.

What I've found is grounding is almost like prayer, a necessary tool to get through life. I can't go through life without praying, as it is the same as grounding. I have learned to see grounding as a part of my daily routine, just like brushing my teeth in the morning and before bedtime.

HEART LOCKER #7

Forgiveness is giving up the hope
things could have been different.

Not only were the heart chakra clearings important but keeping the second chakra clear of energy was also a necessity.

Like other women in their forties concerned about fertility and having children one day, a few years ago, I was told carrying my own children would be extremely dangerous due to underlying health conditions, which included my hypertension diagnosis when I was twenty.

I had spent most of my life working my way through the many challenges and roadblocks I encountered. There were times I wondered what would have happened if I had done things differently and put a family before my spiritual development. Everyone's life path is different. My path was that of enlightenment and I chose to do so on my own. For now, I am content to dote on my niece, who will be two years old by the time this book is completed.

Once I turned forty, I began searching for more organic ways to preserve my eggs, absent IVF and egg cryopreservation. Due to the cost, neither route was an option for me. I searched for meditations and nonconventional ways to preserve the vitality and health of my ovaries. As I continued WORKING WITH SPIRITS, I was led or even directed to a meditation modality: *the female creative energy.*

Diagram 5.

Mentoring Session from 8/2015
Running your female creative energy primarily
for 2nd chakra cleansing and protection.

3rd chakra

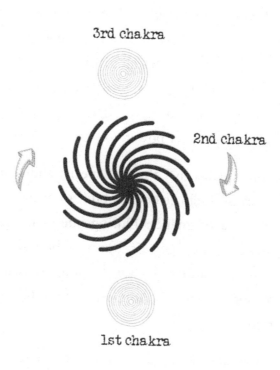

2nd chakra

1st chakra

1. Create a strong grounding cord to the center of the Earth.

2. Visualize a windmill or fan turning on in your pelvic area.

3. Visualize spinning it clockwise.

4. Visualize or imagine foreign energy spinning out of your pelvic area.

Primarily this meditation is used in creating babies but can be helpful as an energy healing and protection tool. It also can be used in the third chakra to help women feel in their own power.

This meditation functions almost like a windmill for manifesting and holding a healing frequency in the female reproductive area. It's almost like meditating; you visualize spinning, bright, high-vibration energy in a windmill formation clearing foreign energy out and help the female body *own* her power.

My mentor explains that this is a special ability only for women, because a female body is built to bring in creator energy during a pregnancy. During one of my personal healing sessions, an energetic bunny rabbit showed up and started drumming. It was helping to maintain a healthy frequency and a continuous flow of healing light in my uterus.

Then, I gradually focused on the other energy ports, synchronizing them to my heart chakra. The meditations of the fourth chakra were like a form of self-healing.

Absolutely, Dr. Albright taught me the body does have the ability to heal *itself*. Once I mastered that lesson, then came a new change and an ending I was not prepared for, nor did I see coming. And like my beloved Romani dancer, there came a day when Dr. Albright was gone, too.

Dr. Albright was a skilled healing guide with so much wisdom. With the potential heart condition averted, we had completed our mission. Just before our last meeting, he shared these words:

"When you find the love and light that's in your heart focus on that. Don't focus on what's wrong, find what's right and expand on it. With every heartbeat is a chance at a new beginning. When you focus on what's wrong it expands. Focus on expanding the light with in you. Focus on expanding the light within your heart."

benevolent galactic beings

One morning I woke up and did my daily meditation and chakra grounding only to notice my friendly spirit guides were not present. I went into the kitchen to fix breakfast, hoping one of them would pop in and say hello. There was nothing—just silence. Glaring, pin-dropping silence. For some reason, I did not immediately panic or think it was odd. Of course, I was used to my guides showing up in the morning or anytime to say hello. But this day, sometime in 2018, was very different. I didn't see any of them, only Yemaya. I knew I had a session with my energy healer later in the day, and I figured I would just check in with my guides then, proceeding with my daily routine.

The healing session came and went and none of my usual friends showed themselves. I began to think, *Is our soul contract coming to an end? Did they move on because I completed another level of ascension?* I assumed there was a new group coming into my life. Was I ready for this? I had no idea the magnitude of what was about to happen. And for the first time, I had a visitation from an off-world being. Yes, off-world as in from another world, another dimension. But I'll come back to this in a minute.

I was very confused and wanted badly for my guides to stay in my life. However, I thought maybe their position in my life had changed. During the session with my mentor none of the usual spirits I worked with showed up, and that's when it all made sense. I didn't recall it at first, but at the end of the session, it all came together. Only then did I remember: the sendoff.

In my dream state the night before, I was in a movie theater with all the spirit guides I worked with at the time. The interesting part was I was on stage looking at them sitting in the audience in front of me. I wasn't aware of what was going on, but then I understood they were moving on. There were no words spoken between any of us. It was just a feeling from them: "*So long! Job well done, and now, off to your next level of ascension.*" All of the helpers left my life, except for Yemaya. Afraid one day she would move on too, I asked her to promise she would never leave my side, and she did.

Once I made peace with the changes in my spirit team, I did my best to quickly adjust to my new situation and what was about to happen. At first, all I saw were bright lights. I couldn't really make out a figure; it was as though I was just looking at pure energy, a healing and high-vibration frequency of light. I have no words to describe the essence of these beings I started working with.

Some of my new friends came from the fourth dimension, and other beings came from the fifth dimension. There are many dimensions outside of time and space beyond earth, these beings told me. However, this was the first group to contact me. I affectionately, and with their permission, refer to them as the Starlight Group. They are a collective consciousness that work together to help mankind, especially those already on a path toward spiritual ascension. Because of my work towards enlightenment, I have spent years developing my intuition and coming into a vibration high enough to communicate with these beings. I was told certain off-world beings will speak with those individuals ready to make a change in their life, I felt blessed to have had this experience.

Initially, I was scared, as I could never see a clear image. Many times, I just felt their presence. Sometimes I would see a silhouette of energy forming in front of me. Other times, they would share information with me telepathically and I could feel the downloads in my head, primarily in my crown and third eye chakras. The downloads felt like soft ocean waves that cover your feet when you're walking on the beach or a warm breeze that bounces off your face, in the summertime. I didn't have to force these gentle feelings; it was effortless.

Sometimes I would see soft layers of silver light and I would just feel the changes as they came in; there was no discomfort. Most times the contact would start while I was doing meditations. I cannot stress how important, how relevant, grounding is to your spiritual development. From personal experience, I have found that when I'm not grounded, the information from spirits or high-dimensional beings does not come in clearly, and I have trouble receiving the information. With no cord, I couldn't maintain a connection to the earth, my mind would not feel balanced, and day-to-day activities would be difficult to complete. Now, I hope I have really, really, REALLY stressed the importance of maintaining a grounding cord! Just refer back to (Diagram 1) as a reference point.

I've always looked forward to reading the horoscope section in magazines at the beginning of the month. I believe this Starlight Group made first contact with me during a Saturn and Mercury retrograde, meaning both planets were rotating in the opposite direction.

Mercury being the planet of communication and Saturn the planet of change, both of them spinning "backwards" created much confusion in my head.

Because I was at the beginning of a new and very intense growth period, the addition of these planets moving counterclockwise would at times cause me to lose confidence in my own ability to speak with these beings.

The planetary shift going on concurrently with this new cycle of growth made me question the life choices and decisions I had made thus far.

Mostly, I thought, *What direction do I want to continue in?* It was as though none of my past experiences had prepared me for the changes I was rapidly making with my new guides and within myself. I couldn't draw on past karmic experiences; I felt I was being given the opportunity to completely set myself free and I was no longer connected to those old experiences. I had transcended them, and as a reward, my internal frequency had elevated enough to match a level of communication with these off-worlders. I was walking into a different vibration to bring me closer with God and these beautiful beings.

These new helpers connected to me and shared information using a silver frequency. It was a higher level of ascension, one I could not make with my past spirit guides. It was so new, so different, I wasn't sure how or if I *could* function in that new vibration. It was a pure, loving energy, unlike anything I had ever encountered before. I did my best to quickly incorporate and adjust to this new way of "chatting."

These light beings called this energy simply "Starlight." It was a vibration new to planet earth but one that is known in other worlds and other planets inhabited by people living there with an elevated consciousness.

The Starlight Group told me I was entering a high-dimensional growth cycle.

As a collective consciousness, they showed themselves as a unity of one.

I was fortunate I had a skilled and seasoned mentor to help me communicate with these 5D beings. This group explained in their own words, *"We are ancient and always. An energy consciousness. We have a thread of light that goes back to the origin of everything. We encompass all dimensions."*

In addition to the Starlight Group, another type of 5D beings began connecting with me. Another group consciousness, the Pleiadeans. Both explained there had been a major shift, a major planetary realignment and upgrade. My first experience with the Pleiadeans was that of **responsibility**. They stressed the importance of being aware of the choices I made that could affect my health, my mind, and my spiritual evolvement—everything.

Personal accountability, as they called it, was of the utmost importance in spiritual development.

Up to this point, I had relied on my healing guides to "fix me up" when I suffered from different ailments or if I felt stuck mentally or spiritually.

Now, I was being motivated to take the helm and steer the ship for myself.

Was I nervous? Absolutely. Did I want my spirit guides back in my life? Of course. Did I feel I was ready for this next level of ascension? Well, it would seem I was already going through the process, and therefore I had to make quick changes to manage the information being shared with me.

I have never thought of having control of my life and personal empowerment in a spiritual sense. On a physical level, sure, I knew I had the power to control what went in and what came out of my mouth. I knew my thoughts could manifest physically. However, I never realized my mind could affect each cell in my body at the DNA level.

The information shared from these high-dimensional beings changed my idea of the relationship between my mind and my body. It was a whole new way of thinking for me. The idea that I could talk to my own cells, my DNA, and both would respond to my intentions to be healthy. This were the first teachings from the Pleiadeans.

Eventually, when I would begin to have feelings and symptoms of pain or an illness forming, I would talk to my body and say: "*Do what you need to do to heal, to be in balance, to be healthy.*" In the beginning, when I first started working with the Pleiadeans and the Starlight Group, their vibrations were so intense, I needed the assistance of my energy healer to help channel the information.

Over time, I was able to develop a connection that allowed me to have more direct communication with them. Patience has not been one of my stronger personality traits, but I've gotten better with that over time! That old saying " Haste makes waste" is so true. I took my time developing a relationship with these two galactic groups and gradually, they taught me how to improve the body-to-spirit connection.

They wanted me to rely more on my own internal intuition as opposed to someone else's judgment. They also stressed that mankind or humanity was gradually waking up and becoming more amenable to working with spirits and galactic beings. I believe we are all on the cusp of a new energy dynamic forming on the earth. I believe this awakening started with mankind searching for a deeper connection to God and their own spirituality. This change inspired me to share my experiences with those willing to listen and to accompany me on this journey, this spiritual evolution.

Mentoring Session 7/2018
Pleiadean Healing Meditation

1. Create a strong grounding cord to Earth.
2. Visualize yourself inside a sphere of light.
3. Visualize this energy sphere around your body from all sides and top to bottom.
4. Then ask a Pleiadean guide to come and assist you in healing yourself.

The Starlight Group also helped me focus on my wants and not so much on my needs. Sometimes we all get trapped in life and tend to focus solely on our responsibilities. Over time our passions get pushed to the side, and then we forget about them. I was told the heart chakra is also the connection to the celestial world. This makes sense since this has been the area of most healing for me.

The Starlight Group showed me a symbol around and over my fourth chakra. This configuration covered most, if not all, of that area. They explained it was an energetic limitation created by my thoughts. This was another example of how my mind had shaped and created my reality. That mechanism formed because I was obsessed with the idea of working and doing what I needed to pay my bills, while my heart was leaning in another direction.

As a medical technologist and clinical microbiologist, I had worked in a few laboratories. It was a great source of inspiration for me, as I love figuring things out. I even used to play detective when I was little. Over time, though, my interests started to change. There were days I would have liked to be on the other side of the phone when giving lab results. Then I considered changing my job to do another kind of research.

At the time, I thought I needed a vacation. I had been working so much, with few to no breaks with multiple respiratory viruses affecting society, that

I needed a reboot and to feel motivated again. I had spent over twenty years in the clinical research field, and my interest was no longer the same. Just before the start of 2019, these ideas started to form in my head: *Am I ready to move into more of a teaching role now? Am I ready to share my own research protocols? Is it possible to create clinical trials that enhance the patient care experience with a 5D perspective?*

I knew I was being guided by these off-worlders into an area that would make my heart sing again. There were so many ideas manifesting in my mind when we communicated. From that point on they were my friends, the BENEVOLENT GALACTIC BEINGS. And for the first time in a long time, I started to feel in charge of my life again.

forgiveness & acceptance

E ven though my spirit guides were no longer present, I had these benevolent galactic beings helping me to continue the ascension process. A new group of celestial beings, or angels, as I referred to them, started to connect with me. As I ascended, the healing guides I worked with came from a higher energy vibration as well. Usually this happened when I went into a meditative phase.

I would choose a quiet time, usually when I came home from work in the morning and I just got out of the shower. I would sit on the floor in my living room, ground (page 27) and then start the Spinning vortex meditation™ (page 67) or Blowing roses meditation (page 111) to clear my space and mind of distractions. Soon I would start to feel or even see small beams of energy. Sometimes I would hear information coming from my new guides.

Once I was done meditating and the guides departed, I would then quickly write a text message to myself on my phone and then self-email it, to make sure I didn't lose the information. They encouraged me to share the most important lesson I have learned through this healing process.

This twenty-year growth period allowed me to acquire enlightenment; some lessons were very harsh, and some were very loving. However, the most profound lesson to date was and has been that of *forgiveness*. This book was nearly all but completed and I was encouraged to return to the writing process by my guides and share my own personal experiences about this topic.

Here are the words of these angelic messengers: *"We come wanting to possibly help you and other people see forgiveness and acceptance in a new way. To help mankind see this concept in a different way. To transcend the present-day idea. Some people add their own judgment. I'll forgive you, if you deserve to be forgiven. I'm bestowing forgiveness on you because I can. Some people aren't really giving forgiveness, it's just words coming from the person's ego."*

Honestly, FORGIVENESS has not been my strongest asset. Without any doubt and somewhat giving myself the side-eye, I admit it has always been a challenge for me. I've never been good at just "letting go," especially when another person's actions have caused me harm. Well, where should I start? What example should I first expand on? What experience in my life do I feel is **un**forgiveable? I think it's obvious. I wrote about it in the first few chapters.

To this day I am still struggling with the idea and thoughts of *How much more could I have accomplished in my life if I hadn't been deliberately held back? Could I have gone further in life?* I get upset when I think this way. And so, I try not to think this way, but in a better way :

I do my best to remember how far I've come in my life.

I do my best to think about how much I have accomplished.

I do my best to be thankful I'm still on the earthly plane.

I do my best to be and remain in a frequency of gratefulness.

I do my best to remember the universe has allowed me to live forty-seven years.

I do my best to really appreciate that I'm still alive.

No matter what has happened to me in the past, I'm still here, living and breathing and doing the best I can. Has it always been easy? Absolutely not!

But I'm here; thank God I'm still here. And I'm surviving despite what I've been through. Now, these angelic messengers guided my hand, and directed me as I wrote this part of my journey.

Trust me, I was not willing, not ready, to share this part of my story. As I put pen to paper, it was and is very cathartic. It's a challenge and makes me feel vulnerable. I'm sure some reading this would think, *Ah! But you have shared so much already.*

Yes, I have shared quite a bit about my life. However, giving someone a clean slate is an ability—to this day—I continue to work on. Absolutely, I know and have learned it's really all about me. Moving on from a situation has really nothing to do with other people. But it's still difficult at times. What right did anyone have to think they could play GOD with someone's time on earth ? What right did anyone have to feel they could control what direction I took in my life?

It was my path; my choices and my options were stolen from me! And several others, in fact, attempted to derail me, and in some cases, blatantly tried to control my ability to make decisions for myself.

Yes, this is the hot topic: FORGIVENESS.

Does anyone **not** struggle with this at times? I don't know one person who has not encountered an experience in their life when they felt, *I'm done with you and all your drama.*

And you know what? Sometimes it must be that way, especially when dealing with another person unwilling to change or heal themselves. As I wrote before, and it's also one of my heart lockers—number seven to be exact— it's not forgetting what the other person did or did not do.

It's letting go of the hope you could change things. The focus is moving into acceptance and making sure that that experience will not have an effect anymore.

There will be challenges along the way; I'm working through some new experiences and setbacks as I complete this chapter. The trick is to remain balanced while I'm going through the lesson, not taking it personally and being patient with myself.

Now I recall, back in the early 1990s, Ms. Cee Cee once said to me during a mentoring session, "The world is full of people who couldn't make it in hell and couldn't make it in heaven.

Didn't belong in hell and didn't belong in heaven. And so, you are here to learn to ascend and know you can call on the angels for support and protection." Amazingly, I remembered her words just as I was writing this passage, just like it was yesterday.

The best way to transcend pain and move past hard times begins with a balanced perspective. Not just for others and their actions—but mostly for *myself*.

In the past, I would be so quick to just cut someone out of my life if they wronged me or caused some type of emotional trauma. Giving them a second chance was the last thought in my mind. I had such a high expectation of others and myself. The pattern I followed all my life until recently was the "cut and run" concept. I wouldn't bother to address or heal issues that I faced; I would just cut the person off, end communication and move into a new problem to deal with. That method never worked.

I had to learn to be sympathetic of where other people are in their own growth cycle. That would then allow me to interact with them without having expectations or wanting them to be different. That's called **compassion**.

When I thought about Jesus, I remembered he loved everybody, no matter what they did. That kind of mastery is what moving on is really all about. I was in the process of clearing negative thought patterns, like taking unwanted clothes off the rack in my bedroom closet.

In the past, there were times when I would have a snap reaction to certain behaviors. Sometimes I would reach a certain level with a person and just say, "I'm done, done with that nonsense," and close the door on them, that was it. I've since changed this behavior.

There are many modalities and paths to starting over with someone. It could happen with family members, coworkers or even in personal relationships.

So, what about FORGIVENESS in love affairs? I will be the first to admit this has been a delicate subject for me. Because I haven't been willing to accept the blame for things I did or said wrong, my romances haven't been the best. I did not always make the best choices in affairs of the heart. That mainly stemmed from my inability and lack of empathy for someone else's behavior. Not giving the other person the chance to go through their own ascension, not giving them the time. They just needed to "figure things out." Let me explain a bit more.

For a very long time, I was on a never-ending search for the perfect partner. The reality is there is no flawless person in the world. Everyone has their own cycles of change, growth, testing and renewal to experience.

Unconsciously, I expected my partners to be patient with me and the changes I was going through, but I was not able to do the same for them.

That's what the universe does sometimes. It will take us on a journey and introduce us to a new person. I would get to know them, then I would think, *I don't prefer that type of personality or trait. I want someone better.* Then someone else would come along and now it was, *I don't prefer that aspect either.* Every relationship became a step closer to what I really wanted and what was best for me.

I was looking for a loving, healthy relationship where I was appreciated for who I was, but I was the person who did not allow other people to be themselves. How could I attract a healthy relationship with someone who accepted me when I obviously was not a vibrational match? The universe had taken me through relationships to help me become more receiving of myself and others.

What happened? I ended up going through a few relationships where someone was critical of me or I was critical of them, until I came to this realization: This idea of judging and trying to mold someone to be like I want them to be, was not working. How could I shift my perception or reality? I realized I needed to learn about ACCEPTANCE.

Once I became more embracing of myself and raised my vibrational frequency then I would be a match for what I was looking for. This path may happen quickly for some people. They change a little and meet their right partner immediately. Others, like me, change slowly and meet different people along the way, while they continue changing to get a healthier way of thinking.

And what is FORGIVENESS without ACCEPTANCE?

Allowing a person to be who and what they were at that specific time in their life and not letting it affect my path to enlightenment was important. And this in no way means giving anyone permission to continue with misconduct or to take advantage—not at all.

Similar to the issues that began with my heart, the slight murmur that developed, other areas of my body also showed signs of a potential health issues. In early 2015, I suffered from different levels of pain in my eyes and joints.

I would just dismiss the pain as, alright, I need to lose more weight or maybe I walked too fast up those stairs or put too much pressure on this part of my foot. I would make any excuse not to visit the doctor's office. I would do online research and decide this is what illness I had or maybe I had something similar. Self-diagnosing is not something I would recommend anyone attempt unless they are qualified to do so.

In 2016, when that pain escalated to the formation of chronic inflammation, I knew there was something else behind the dis-EASE. I started to focus on the spiritual part and what I found was a combination of issues.

It wasn't just a physical influence to the soreness in my eyes, but there was a spiritual effect as well. It all went back to my thoughts. When the "episodes" started to occur, I was simultaneously working through a new growth cycle.

This inflammation was my body holding and storing pain, disappointment, judgment, and non-forgiveness from past experiences. It could then express them as a physical disease like osteoarthritis in some people, or in my case, a mild version of rheumatoid arthritis.

I'll go step by step here:

On the earthly plane I was dealing with chronic uveitis, which is inflammation in the eye. It would come and go, flare up and then calm down and later spread to the interior parts which then required medication in the form of steroid drops, prescribed by my doctor. Of course, I went through several clinical tests to determine the root cause and my test results came back "inconclusive" or no obvious reason.

During energy healing sessions with my mentor and healing guides, they all explained the burning sensation and cloudiness in my eye had become a physical manifestation of my stubborn nature.

WHAT DID I DO TO COMBAT THIS PROBLEM?

1. be less judgmental.
2. forgive, give up the idea things could be different.
3. accept that that's where that person is in life and I don't have to participate in their story; I'm only obligated to heal myself.
4. meditate—use the blowing roses technique.
5. show compassion and move on!

Mentoring Session 8/2019
Blowing Roses to release judgment

1. Create a firm grounding cord to Earth.
2. Visualize creating roses.
3. Imagine the concept of judgment inside those roses.
4. Visualize exploding those roses, releasing any judgment, you placed inside them then send it down to mother Earth.

On a side note, when I had the flare-ups in my eyes, I did research and found following a gluten-free eating regimen also helped. I tried these foods and surprisingly there were fewer periods and eventual remission of the uveitis. However, if I returned to eating regular foods too often, I again would have to deal with the pain and redness.

My point is, there are many ways to combat the visible effects of judgment and the best way is through FORGIVENESS and ACCEPTANCE. Believe me, it's not easy. I have spent more than twenty years learning this lesson, but it works. And it was not for the other person's benefit—it was for my benefit.

I recall a movie I watched a few years ago. A mother was talking to her daughter about moving on after she had suffered a betrayal in a relationship—the loss of her marriage, being thrown out of her marital home and having to start over with nothing.

I remember the mom explaining, "When a person hurts you, it's like they take power over you. You hold a grudge, they keep the power." I'm paraphrasing, but I hope the concept and idea are clear.

In my opinion FORGIVENESS is letting go. ACCEPTANCE is giving up trying to change the other person and releasing the need to pass judgment. I ascended to a neutral space of compassion and sensitivity.

I think we all have moments of what I call our own "personal craziness," or our issues that need to be worked on. Until I learned to welcome someone unconditionally, I couldn't move on from the situation, the hurt feelings and being taken advantage of. I would stay stuck in my anger. This went on for years, until my idea of how I wanted to live a happy life changed.

Instead of walking around in my angry space, I would think to myself. *That was an abusive situation and I'm out of it now. I don't need to create my life or share my energy around that memory anymore.*

I had this long-established thought pattern, *I have to create my life through pain.* Someone once even said to me, "You learn through suffering," but I did not want to believe that! I had to energetically remove this concept—thank goodness for the blowing roses meditation. My belief is that learning comes after a difficult situation, not so much in the process. When it ended, then I took a step back and saw the lessons in the experience.

We do have a choice in how we compose our reality. We can build a challenging life full of pain or a fun life that is more enjoyable.

So, to close—letting go of a situation does not mean tolerating bad behavior. ACCEPTANCE doesn't mean allowing abuse, it means acknowledging the current situation and then going forward to live my best life, with FORGIVENESS and compassion.

HEART LOCKER #8

Always live in the present moment.
The moment of *now*.

radiant heart

The new friendships I formed with all my galactic friends, helped me continue the growth and ascension process. The challenge now was to find a way to connect both realities, the 3D and 5D planes, and have them coexist.

I decided to find a way to walk in both realms, connecting through the fourth chakra. Everything has its origin at the heart center and its ability to hold and balance the frequency of love.

I learned the hard way that my thoughts were the gateway to both positive and negative experiences in my life. If I was holding on to hurt, pain, and judgments, it affected my heart and its frequency, and the end result was discomfort. Of course, I had my quarterly checkups with my doctor, due to my high blood pressure. However, there was monitoring I needed to do on a spiritual level as well. My mind and body were influencing each other; both seemed to be intertwined. Once I decided to share this journey, I felt I needed to reflect on where I started and what I learned.

There are eight main points and I will explain each one step-by-step:

1. GROUND YOURSELF

I needed to do my best to always stay grounded. Without that cord between me and mother earth, it would be a challenge to stay functional in life, in work, in spiritual evolvement, and with family and friends. More importantly, without that special connection, it was a challenge to stay in tune with myself. One of my problems in the past was being able to distinguish my wants from my needs.

In some ways, I was obsessive-compulsive. I had trouble making simple decisions, from what type of clothes to wear to what screen saver I should have on my laptop. Once I started the meditations, that indecision and confusion dissipated over time. Those "episodes," as I call them, became few and far between. I started listening to the guidance coming from my heart rather than the information coming from my head. How did I learn to know the difference between the two?

Well, having a grounding cord to Earth helps a great deal, and being in line to the divine source or the universe helped the most. And by "source," I mean whatever you choose to believe is of a higher nature. For me, it's God or my higher self—they are all the same energy consciousness. For others, it may be someone or something else.

2. CREATE YOUR REALITY

What I needed to make my heart sing again was so simple yet almost unattainable. "Dare to dream that you can have what you truly want," I would hear my guides telling me. Because of past experiences, I would hear these ideas run through my head: *Oh, it's okay if I don't get what I want or something close to it* or *It just wasn't meant to be.* Meanwhile, the universe was telling me, "No, you can have what you want—you can create your own path in life, you can have a position that makes your heart sing again."

Sometimes, I felt I needed to protect myself by believing what I was trying to manifest wouldn't happen. That way, there would be no disappointment. The opposite, however, was the truth. The more I believed, the more ideas happened in the real world. As I wrote earlier, our thoughts shape and create our reality. Positive thoughts create pleasant experiences, and negative thoughts create difficult experiences. The only way you get what you want is because you believe you deserve it, whatever that may be. I began to clear the beliefs within myself that said, *You can't have what you want.* Then, my ability to create things became easier. I also started removing this long-held thought system where I believed getting what I wanted depended on other people. No longer would I give my power away. I started to focus on what type of life I deserved and not worry about how the universe would make it happen.

3. SHOW COMPASSION

There was a restrictive feeling I had in my fourth chakra relating to fear. To deal with any feelings of doubt, my guides encouraged me to focus on the idea of compassion. There was this old energy dynamic where I would confuse someone else's pain as my own, and I would absorb their hardships as a way to help them. That behavior is called "the wounded healer approach." I did this so much in the past that it then caused imbalance in my own heart chakra. I had to upgrade to an energy dynamic most helpful to myself and other people. No more would I step into someone else's darkness or negative experiences. I learned to stand in my light and help them from a place of strength.

4. LOVE IS THE ANSWER

As this ascension process continued, I would notice sometimes when my breathing was difficult, all I needed to do was open up to the vibration of love. We all have this ability. And how did I do that? I accomplished this by using the meditations I wrote about earlier. Now, my focus was to dissolve and move out any foreign energy not meant to be there. The more I balanced the expansion of love, the easier life in general became. When I live without judgment, I live in peace. I learned to handle any emotional pain by asking my soul to spread love throughout my heart chakra, to radiate it throughout my entire system.

5. LOOK FOR THE ANSWERS WITHIN

I was searching for a light outside of myself. All these years, I had been looking for answers I already had. That bond to God had always been there. There was a common theme through all my experiences. Unconditional love for myself and others. Energetically, I could feel my soul cracking my chest open with love, and that's when my true-life path became clear. I found myself at the end of this twenty-year growth process and at the doorsteps of a new one. It began with sharing this road to enlightenment, writing about my journey, and encouraging those ready to join the path of their own awakening.

6. LET GO OF THE PAST

When I wrote about a developing heart murmur, it related also to a pattern of thought. In spite of my various healing sessions, I was still holding on to difficult chapters of my life. These thoughts had become like snake venom in my body and within my soul. There was a karmic script that was beginning. When we avoid healing past traumas, circumstances will force us to deal with those realities.

Because of my history—verbal abuse, being taking advantage of, etc.—I found I would compartmentalize these incidents inside my heart chakra. If I felt there was someone who could potentially hurt me or make my life difficult, I would not allow them to have access to me. As a result, my heart energetically started to be affected and changed to an appearance of a walnut shell with little "rooms." This caused my fourth chakra to seem segmented and blocked. Instead, what I needed to do was open my heart and allow the energy to flow uninhibited. Ultimately, it was up to me to remove any restrictions.

Because I had opened my life to people in the past who took advantage, I then believed the best form of protection was to close myself off to them. And by doing so, that energy put me in a state of resistance and created those harmful energetic formations. It was a long pattern of behavior for me. This murmur my doctor heard was my body giving me a heads-up.

I needed to change the way I lived and not live with the chronic theme of "I have to fight my way through life." With the assistance of my guides and mentor, I was able to change the way I had lived. They explained the best protection was actually to have my heart completely open and flowing freely. Then, I would be vibrating at a high frequency of love, and this was the best form of protection. They went on to explain that anyone who comes along, not equal to that energy frequency could not coexist and would leave me alone.

7. RAISE YOUR VIBRATIONS

The Pleiadeans went on to teach me ways to raise my vibrational frequency on all levels of my reality and helped me distinguish the ideas coming from my higher self versus the ideas coming from my ego. They helped me peel away layers of protection around my chest that said, "It's not safe to be in a vibration of love." I had lived the majority of my life in a state of defensiveness. They helped me to change this idea to a more balanced way of thinking. I was stuck in a train of thought, this backstory that played and replayed over and over in my head: When I was six years old, this happened. When I was twenty, that happened. When I turned twenty-six, my family member said this or that.

The Pleiadeans explained these were all past-time moments, and they created an energy signature. Most times, it was a harmful energy pattern that began to harden and affect my spiritual well-being. Living in a vibration of acceptance and forgiveness was beneficial both spiritually and physically.

I was also given a loving message from the Starlight Group. I will always remember they were the first off-world beings to communicate with me.

They were just as wise and just as loving as the Pleiadeans.

As I began turning my journal, or journey, into book form, they shared this:

> *"Everything has a heartbeat. The planet has a rhythm the planet has a heartbeat; the Milky Way has a rhythm the Milky Way has a heartbeat. Everything pulses like the heart like the breath in and out."*

8. STAY IN THE NOW

Finally, the most significant lesson I learned is how important the "now" is and can be in every moment. Now doesn't have to carry the story of past hurts. The Pleiadeans explained I had the ability to reset my energy in the present moment and be free of past baggage. And it's not a process that happens overnight. Remember this book is based on more than twenty years of healing work. They were inviting me to ascend, to live and exist in a frequency free of my childhood wounds.

The similarities in my healing sessions were profound. All the pieces had come together like a jigsaw puzzle. The difficulties I've had in my life—the tough lessons, tough lessons, and more tough lessons—they all had the same message, a common theme. Every experience circled back to love: living and existing in a healing frequency of love, maintaining that high vibration and keeping my heart open.

I was excited. I felt like I had completed, what seemed to be the first part of a stairway. *And where is it going?* I ask myself. I can only shrug my shoulders and think, *I guess only time will tell.* But for now, I'm so grateful to have finally found my way back to a RADIANT HEART.

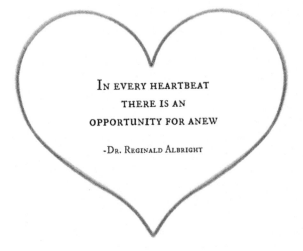

IN EVERY HEARTBEAT
THERE IS AN
OPPORTUNITY FOR ANEW

-DR. REGINALD ALBRIGHT

glossary

aura – your personal energy signature, surrounding your entire being.

botanica – a religious shop that sells herbs, charms and supplies.

chakra – the different energy ports.

karma/karmic – debts that we owe, or someone owes you.

mishigas – a Yiddish term for confusion, craziness

ocha – those who have gone through the initiation process and have been crowned with an orisha; Santero(a)s.

orisha(s) – saints of the Santeria religion.

trabajo – negative energy sent or done to another person through the dark arts; witchcraft.

afterword

To my mentor, ascended masters, life coach, energy healers and all the benevolent galactic beings that helped bring this book to life thank you.

This would not have happened if not for all your guidance, motivation, and support. I feel like all of you were there every step of the way and through the entire process.

Thank You So Much
{{ hugs }}

Special thanks to these artists:

Cover artwork by
CA Pierce

Interior illustrations by
Charlotte Thomson

Meditation sketches by
Niomi Nicci

" *Now you have a beautiful, bright crystal. It wouldn't be so beautiful and bright if it were not for all the grains of sand you encountered in your life.*

—MS. HILDA

from the author

thank you so much for reading my book.

Niomi

Made in United States
North Haven, CT
07 August 2024

55807692R00083